Rumi
Dancing the Flame

Rumi
Dancing the Flame

translations by
Nader Khalili

A celebration of life and love

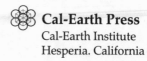

Cal-Earth Press
Cal-Earth Institute
Hesperia. California

Cal-Earth Press is the publishing wing of
Cal-Earth Institute.

The California Institute of Earth Art and Architecture
(Cal-Earth) is dedicated to research and education into the
universal elements of Earth, Water, Air and Fire, their unity
in life - philosophy, poetry, and practice.
Cover: Rumi dome of lights. Hesperia Museum, designed by
architect Nader Khalili and constructed by his apprentices.

Also by the same author:
Racing Alone
Ceramic Houses and Earth Architecture
Sidewalks on the Moon
Rumi, Fountain of Fire

Persian Calligraphy by Ali Heidari
Motifs from the original edition of Rumi's Mathnawi published
by the Konya Museum
Margin Photos of Rumi Dome of Lights, Cal-Earth Institute
Flute player graphic by Maria Jang

For information address: **Cal-Earth Press**
10177 Baldy Lane
Hesperia, CA 92345
FIRST EDITION   email: calearth@aol.com
web page: **www.calearth.org**

Library of Congress Control Number 2001092810

ISBN 1-889625-04 -3

Rumi
Dancing the Flame

translations by
Nader Khalili

Rumi,

for you
who made this
come true

Rumi,

.. the sun, a ball of fire, Rumi's sun, Shams, was rising: One dawn.

("Dreams of Rumi" page 233)

unknown existence
undiscovered beauty
that's how you are
so far
but
one dawn
just like a sun
right from within
you will arise

in this earth
in this earth
in this immaculate field
we shall not plant any seeds
except for compassion
except for love

Rumi,

all the precious words
you and i have exchanged
have found their way
into the heart of the universe
one day they'll pour on us
like whispering rain
helping us arise
from our roots again

1

Dancing the Flame

my essence is the essence
of ruby wine
making my chalice
lament in time
cup after cup
wine after wine
the wine gone into my head
and me into the wine

2

the sweetheart
who is blocking my sleep
demands tears on my knees
throwing me silently
into the waves
changing the water
to liquid sweet

3

Rumi,

the day i distill to a sea
i'll see the sun in every drop
melting with love in every fire
fusing every moment to unite

4

brimming with happiness
every day and night
your voice is a bliss on my heart
when your tune grows tired
i am tired
your voice is a sugarcane
played like a flute

5

whoever is molding your breath
that alone in hard times
will not leave you alone
beaming your heart
with hopeful dreams
finding lovely friends
for your home

6

Rumi,

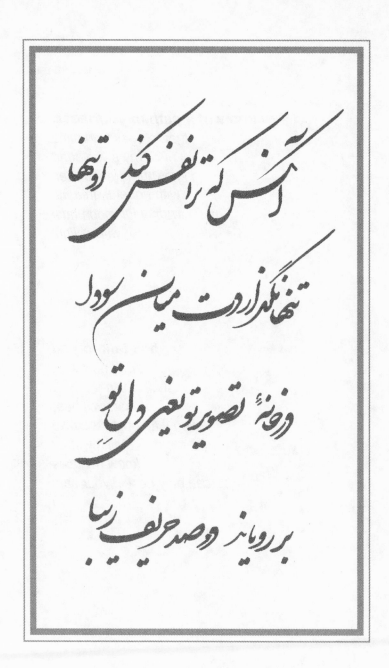

آتش که تو را نفس کند تنها

تنها نگذارد و تو میان سودا

در خنه‌ی تصویر تو نگین دل تو

بر رویاند و صد حرف زیبا

i know of a path in your heart
that merges with mine
my sweetheart
i know of a tranquil sea
within me
that mirrors your moon-face
with delight

7

i shall talk to you
with no words
i shall whisper to you
no ears will hear
even if among the crowd
i tell my story
i know my tales
can only nest in your ears

8

Rumi,

i'm a stranger to be or not to be
walking away from both
is not for a man
with all the turmoil
going on inside me
it's crazy that
i haven't yet gone mad

9

Dancing the Flame

my sweetheart
the idol of ecstasy
sat by my side
filled with nirvana
embracing the
silken string harp
playing the tune
"i am happy
and i am here
without me"
10

Rumi,

it's high time
to be only thinking of you
heating your body
with flame and glow
you are a gold mine
hidden in the earth
to purify you
we must set you
on fire

11

i only see myself
coming and going for you
i only see myself
wishing and looking for you
even if i falter
everywhere in this world
isn't it because
i see nothing but you

12

birds are free from the cage
cage is empty from the birds
where have you flown from
to be so happy
i can smell eternity
in your songs
13

the sweetheart in my dream
last night
had the soul and body
of a silver sea
asking everyone
today as i seek
hoping again to find
longing again to see
14

as long as your path is
lust and greed
every moment your
chance of union is missed
in the journey of quest
if you keep trying
your hope for union
can succeed

15

you wrote a message
on the heart we safekeep
the one you and i
can only read
you promised to reveal
when we're alone
this too we know
what it would mean

16

if you want to be happy
and dwell with me
let go of your
double heartedness and be
then you'll become
you with me as you were
and i'll become
me with you as i was

17

Rumi,

i am so close to you
yet so far
so mixed with you
yet so alone
i've become known
while disguised
so healthy yet
painful inside
18

i wish i knew
who i were
i wish i knew
my share in life
if i could only hear
with clear ear
i would weep for me
with a thousand eyes
19

Dancing the Flame

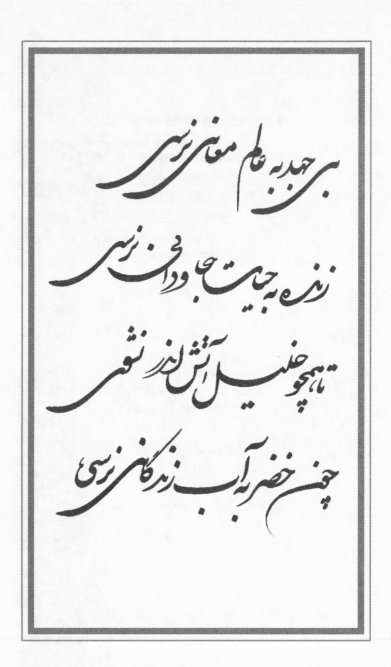

بی جهد به علم معانی نرسی

زنده به حیات جاودانی نرسی

تا همچو خلیل آتش اندر نشوی

چشم خضر آب زندگانی نرسی

Rumi,

you can never arise
without effort
you can never live forever
while you're alive
just like the prophets
unless you enter the fire
you can never find
the water of life
20

you are the letter
written by God
you are the mirror
that reflects the divine
seek inside for
all you want is all you are
there is nothing
above and beyond
21

out there you'll find
dead souls
strange crowds
from East and West
a voice calls you to
follow the source
look inside
and you'll find
a human sea
22

Rumi,

your soul and mine
were one at the roots
our in and out
were one at the heart
i am naive
calling that yours or mine
since me and you
has vanished
from
you and i
23

this love is the owner
of my bread cloth and home
this love has taken
my body eyes and soul
there is one more thing
it's taken away from me
i can't tell
till there is
the right group
place and time
24

take me in my love
take my soul
set me on ecstasy
take both of my worlds
if i rest my heart on
anything but you
throw me with fireball
take everything i hold
25

wake up
let's run wild
in the moonlight
wake up
let's interrupt
the sleep of narcissus
we've been sailing on ice
for a long time
it's high time to
venture the waves now
26

Rumi,

all i've asked from you
is you and you again
from your love
i've already spread our feast
i don't remember
what i dreamt last night
all i know is
i woke up drunk
27

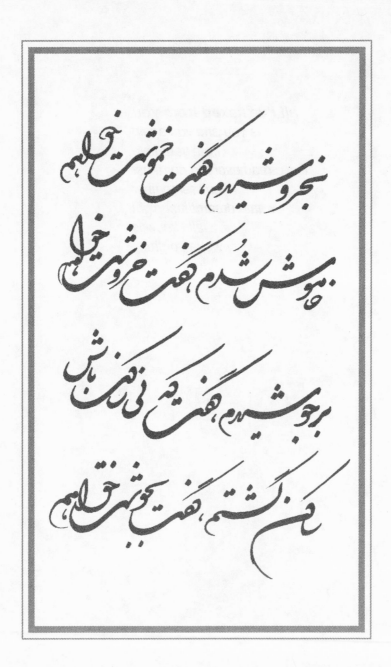

نجبرو شیرم هفت خموشی نی خیام

بهوش شدم هفت خروشی خیا(م)

بر جو شیرم هفت یم نی رنگ باش

نام نگشتم هفت یحوشی خقام

Rumi,

i was in rage
love said be quiet
i kept silence
love said have you no rage
i was on fire
love said go tranquil
i went tranquil
love said have you no fire

28

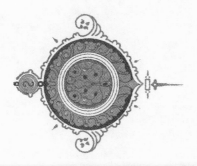

i can't let you know
all the secrets
i can't open to you
all the doors
there is something inside
that makes me happy
but i can't put my finger
on its source

29

Rumi,

you seek this world
you're a mercenary
you yearn for paradise
you've lost the path
since you're happy
in both worlds
as a drifter
you're excused
but you know no pleasure
found in pain

30

how sad that i am alone
in this odd time
sailing in a sea
seeing no shoreline
moving the boat
in a grim dark night
in God's water
with God' s grace
31

come my love
you're that precious sun
without you
living colors
in leaves and gardens
are gone
without you it's all
dust and dark
come my love
my party has no spark

32

i was first seduced by love
then put in a fire of agonies
as i won the mastery
of the beloved
the beloved dropped me
and was gone

33

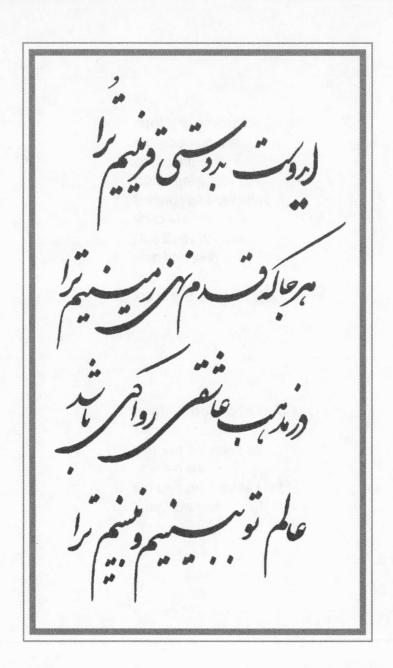

ای دوست بدوستی قرینیم تُرا

هرجا که قدم نهی زمینیم تُرا

در مذهب عاشقی روا کی باشد

عالم تو ببینیم و نبینیم تُرا

Rumi,

sweetheart i see myself
very close to you
like earth
i welcome your every step
is it fair to call you
my entire world
and yet not
find you around

34

i came to this world
riding a horse named love
every night is bright
with ecstasy and delight
since in my religion
the intoxication by
pure wine is allowed
you will never see
my lips gone dried
35

ever since i let you
out of my arms
no one has ever
seen my tearless eyes
for heaven's sake
don't forget me
since you've dwelled
in the soul
heart and
vision of mine
36

Rumi,

those bitter words
that break my heart
surely can never
pour out of your mouth
those sweet lips
spill nothing but tenderness
if there is bitterness
it's only my bad luck
37

it's your voice
making me sing so fine
hearing your call
and i'm generous like God
you've owned me
a hundred times
buy me once more
give me a new life
38

those eyes of yours
teach me divine laws
that love of yours
makes my soul spark
if i'm safe
from evil eyes
it's only because
i'm blessed
by your eyes
39

words are rolling
out of my tongue
without me
someone is ordering
whom i don't know
i wish honey
or poison but
who deserves what share
no one knows
40

Rumi,

as long as i'm with you
i can't sleep
having you
as long as you are away
i can't sleep
crying for you
dear God
i'm sleepless
both nights
but look at the
difference in the
two insomnias

41

love and love alone
that's all i've known
in the beginning, the middle
and to the end unknown
someone is calling me
i think it's my soul
open the door
lazy in love
answer the call

42

Rumi,

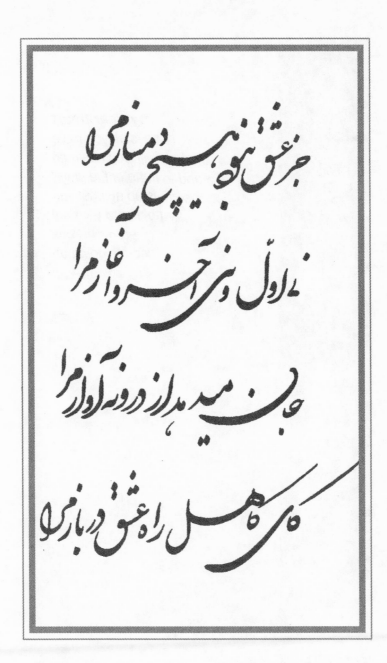

جز عشق تو نیست هیچ دمسازم را

نز اول و نی آخر و آغازم را

جز ناله و ناله از در و غازم را

کآی کاهل راه عشق در بازم را

my dear heart
hope is all you have
don't let it go
if the entire world
is up against you
hold onto your pal
there are wondrous
secrets going on

43

Rumi,

since God had written my life
early in the game
why all the fight and fear
if i were bad
you'll feel relieved
when i'm gone
if i were good
remember
what we have done

44

there is a soul
within your soul
seek it out
there is a treasure
in your mountain
seek it out
a mystic in motion
if that's what you are
don't seek out there
seek inside

45

God will renew your life
when this one is done
your essence remains
when the perishable is gone
love is
the water of life
step inside
every drop
of this sea
holds the promise
of a different life

46

Rumi,

if you want to find yourself
leave yourself alone
wade in no little creek
swim in the big flow
you are that bull
who carries the world
revolt for once
and topple the globe
47

when i die
*hand me over
to my sweetheart
one kiss
on my dead lips
don't be surprised
if i come alive*
48

Rumi,

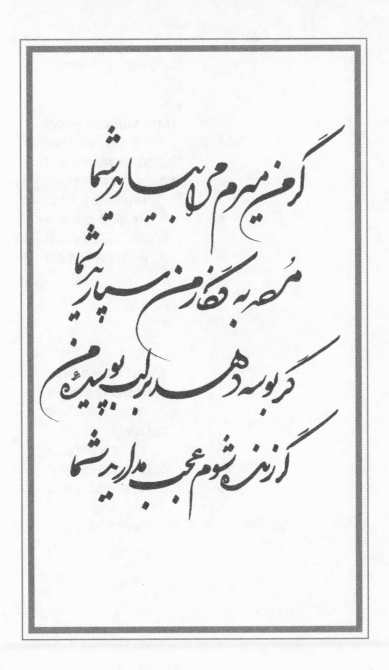

time will cut short
all this glory
this merciless wolf
will cut down the herd
everyone's head
is filled with ego
a flood called death
will wipe it all out

49

there was a time
when my thought
soared as a king
or a time when i mourned
like a prisoner
those days are gone
and i have promised
not to take myself
seriously again

50

Rumi,

i'm a speck of dust
basking in your
sun-like beauty
i'm filled with pain
and you're the healer
no wings yet i fly after you
you are the amber
and i'm merely a straw
changing to a straw
to be pulled by you
51

Mansour was the man
who said he was God
he merely watched
his body depart
he never said
he was God
it was He who said
he was God
52

this earthly body of ours
is the light of the heavens
our agile flights
are the envy of angels
one day the celestial bodies
wish to have our pure souls
one day we are a dare devil
who frightens a monster

53

for awhile
i chose myself to adore
losing me in me
i deserved no more
it seemed i couldn't
see myself
yet i knew
when i stepped out
then me and myself
i beheld

54

Rumi,

__yearn for the bite__
you cannot swallow
search for the knowledge
that doesn't exist
there is a secret
hidden in the heart of holy men
seek that
which God's angel can't
55

today like everyday
i'm in no sober mood
don't open the door
to my thoughts
begin the music instead
for the one who sees
only the beloved's face
there are a hundred
ways to pray
to prostrate
or to be humbled
to the ground

56

Rumi,

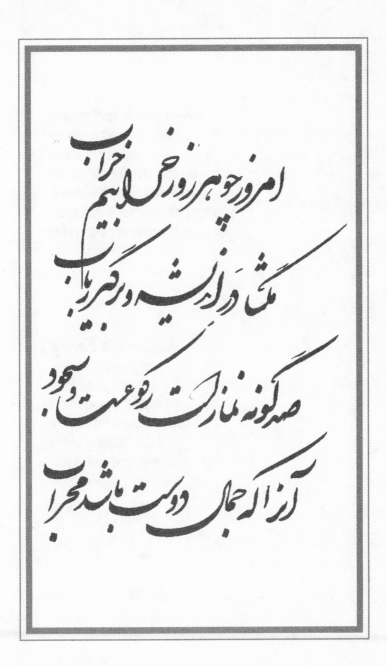

امروز چو هر روز رخ آییم خراب

مگ در اندیشه و در گیر یاب

صد گونه نماز است رکوعهت سجود

آن را که جمال دوست باشد محراب

Dancing the Flame

55

don't think too much
put yourself to sleep
thinking is a veil
on the face of the moon
your heart is like the moon
don't cover it with thoughts
cast your thinking on the water
57

someone's hands
are clapping mine
making me lose
my face and mind
someone's heart is happy
by twisting mine
molding and using me
all the time
58

Rumi,

i imagine marching
to heaven drunk
looking for God
if He is to be found
either my feet
must help me
reach my dream
or i'll lose my head
as i've lost my heart

59

i tell my heart
just for a couple
of nights
up to the dawn
don't go to sleep
don't be like
the moon in the
absence of sun
don't go to sleep
like a bucket
rising from a dark well
keep climbing
till you reach the top
don't go to sleep

60

my beautiful friend
for one night
like the moon
don't go to sleep
like the universe
begin dancing
in orbital round
don't go to sleep
the world is lit up
when we are up
for one night
you hold the lantern
don't go to sleep

61

Rumi,

don't sit still
get up
hurry and
mingle now
a lazy body
either eats
or goes to sleep
there is the sound
of music and dance
in the air
move into the circle
of the enlightened
company now

62

i don't really need wine
to get drunk
i don't really need music
to feel delight
without a wine pal
music and dance
i'm intoxicated
happy and gone

63

Rumi,

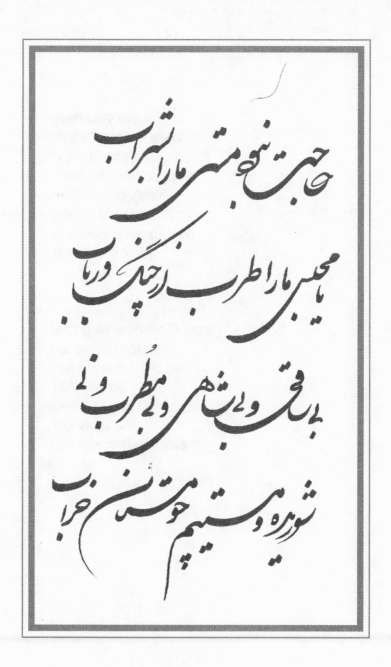

do you hear
the fiddle's surround sound
follow me and
your path will be found
only going astray
you'll find a saintly way
only knowing questions
you'll find a reply
64

good God how is it that
happy as we are
we differ in every way
i'm your luck
never able to go to sleep
you're my luck
never ready to wake up
65

Rumi,

every night i go around town
flowing like water or wind
i can't go to sleep
by wandering around
mind looks for wisdom
in what is defined
don't look for logic
when i'm drunken and gone

66

seek only the knowledge
that un-ties the problems
of your life
seek it soon
before
your number is up
leave alone
what seems to be
but is not
seek what
seems not to be
yet it might

67

Rumi,

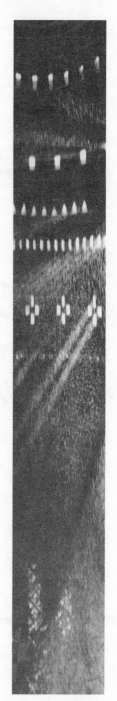

if you seek eternity
don't fall asleep
get into love's fire
don't fall asleep
a hundred nights you slept
and reaped nothing
for God's sake just tonight
don't fall asleep
68

loving my beloved
i'm happy tonight
leaving my worries alone
i'm free tonight
dancing and praying
oh God
let the key to the dawn
be lost tonight
69

Dancing the Flame

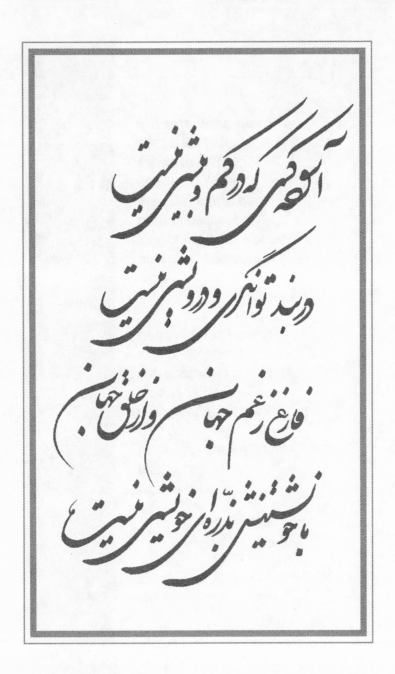

آنکو که نی گر کو ردگم و ثبتی منیت

درند توانگری و درویشی نیت

فارغ ز غم جهان وارستی جهان

با خویشتن نداره ای خوشتری منیت

66   *Rumi,*

happy is the one
who doesn't need to try
getting wealthy
or remaining poor
free from people
and worldly worries
a stranger to himself
free in every way
70

dawn again and morning
is unleashing someone's love
in a magic aroma
enough sleep
the world is leaving
take a deep breath
or the caravan
will take away your share

71

never say
no one knows the way
never say
profound humans
can't be found
just because
you're kept out of
heaven's secrets
you think everyone
is like you

72

Rumi,

i see healing
in every pain
i see compassion
in every rage
on the plains of the earth
and in nine levels
under the dome
of vast heavens
i see only you
in every stage

73

i seek my beloved
restlessly
my life is reaching
to the end
yet i'm still sleeping
suppose i finally
find this beloved
where do you think
i can find my lost life

74

i'm no more just a creature
i'm a pal of God
i refuse to give in
no matter what barrier
or how hard
since his party is filled with
luscious lives and good times
why should i settle
for a life so lukewarm
75

you've finally filled the
world with happiness
the earth and the sky
are thrilled
no one is complaining
any more except
the unhappiness
since you broke
everyone free
from its chains
76

Rumi,

choosing God's path
you'll be agile
and filled with life
beaming once again
back to the heavens
your seat is reserved
way at the top
shame on you settling
like a shadow
on lowly dirt

77

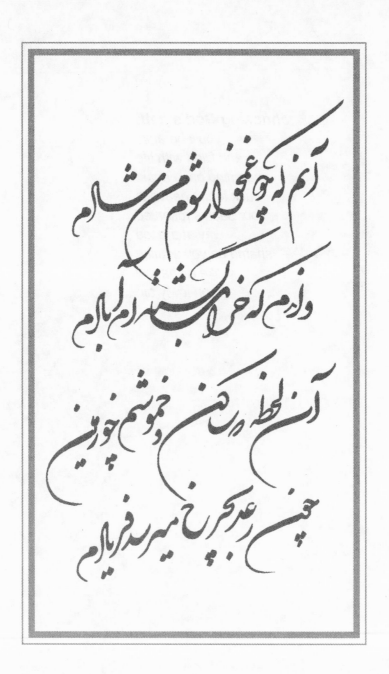

آنم که چو غنچه از غم تو شاد نی‌ام
وانم که چو خار از دل تو شاد نی‌ام

آن لحظه که در کنم خموشم چو زبان
چشم رعد بکرخ می‌رسد فریاد

Rumi,

i am happy
when i am sad
i am together
when fallen apart
like earth
when i am silent
i have thunder
hidden inside

78

the days you seem to be
crazy
you're overflowing
with life
but the days you're
clever and wise
you seem to have
lost the cause

79

in this plentiful
sea of life
with envy and greed
we steal happiness
from each other
a fish never
stores up water
a fish is finished
without the sea

80

in the journey of quest
you must go alone
always be eager
to face the pains
it is not heroic
to hasten for the union
it is heroic
to face the separation

81

Rumi,

come my soul
it's time to go to war
think no more
we have no extra time
this life which is full of farce
at every corner
a hunter or a prey
calls on us to
put on our arms
82

i went to the doctor
a healer of sorts
asked him to hold my pulse
and look at the urine
he said your sickness is
madness mixed with dreams
then leave it alone i said
let it be as long as it is
83

pain and pain and pain
that's your best choice
don't be worried if
luck has left you alone
if you have no pain
then that's the time
to be sad and complain

84

Rumi,

whatever happened between
you and me last night
i can neither write
nor say a word
the day i take my last journey
out of this old country
there will be legend
wrapped around my shroud

85

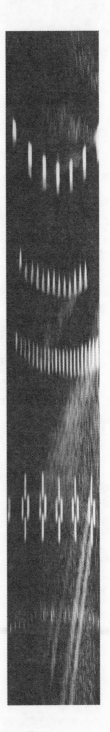

Dancing the Flame

childhood passed
youth was taken away
from the young
now you're old
get ready for the last flight
every guest has a room
for three days reserved
your three days are up
you should be moving on

86

i seek fire
that's my longing for you
i seek a way out
that's how i'm at your door
i'm sick and tired
of being so unhappy
only you can show me
the time of my life

87

Rumi,

شد کودکی در رفت جوانی رجوان

روز پیری رسید بر بر جهان

هر مهمان را سه روز باشد پیمان

ای خواجه سه روز شد تو برخیز و بران

Dancing the Flame

i'm your cure
be patient with pain
i'm your pal
don't look elsewhere
in vain
even if you lose
don't say you've lost
be happy with the race
since i'm your prize

88

wake up my dear heart
the world is speeding away
your share of life
is being wasted away
don't just sleep in the body
or uselessly sit about
the caravan of life
is not waiting around

89

Rumi,

i took a journey
dead set to find
your true love
at any cost
at every stage i landed
i saw a head beheaded
i saw a life is lost
90

if you reach for a star
you are a star
if you try
to make a living
you're merely bread
try to get this
secret message
as your last
you are what you seek
in your future
and the past
91

ah tear drops
brighten my heart
clear the spring blossoms
shining my sight
flowing one night
remembering only
not any indelicate
moments of my life

92

Rumi,

my life was
down into the earth
said a reed flute
suddenly a whimsical hand
beheaded my head
punctured me
over and over
making me a flute
lamenting
ever since i lost my root

93

are you a candle
or a free sufi soul
you have all these six
that show it all
pale and bright
active at night
sleepless
filled with tears
and burning at heart

94

Rumi,

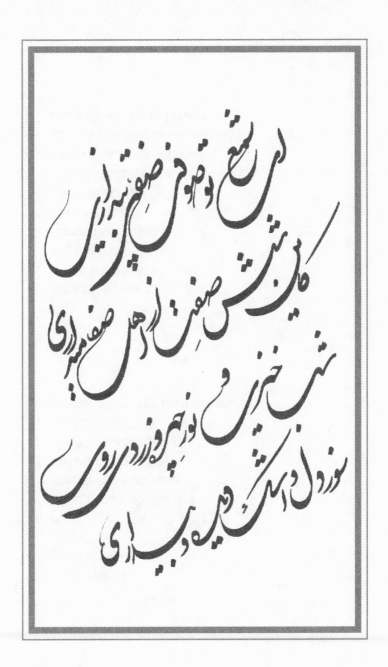

when i first fell in love
my neighbors couldn't rest for
my long lamenting times
now that my lamenting
has gone down
the real love
begins to surface
as high fire
catches on
smoke disappears
95

get up and do some good
for someone now
the universe will surely
safekeep your act
everyone has left his
belongings and is gone
you too
except
for what good
you've done
96

Rumi,

night again
and time to go to sleep
swimming like fish
all day
then sinking deep
next day up again
tending the belongings
i see only God's people
walking His path
97

if you're a seeker
find the company
of seekers
if you're in love
sit by the gate
of those in love
when you've experienced it all
then leave the humans alone
take the company
of no one but God
98

no one exists in this world
except for the one
nothing is ugly or beautiful
known or unknown
but merely that one
every arrow launched
is from the same bow
every word uttered
is from the same tongue
99

i told you don't sit around
with unhappy folks
don't seek the company of any
but those delicious and sweet
when you're in a garden
make your way
around the thorns
seek the company
of narcissus and jasmine
every flower and more
100

Rumi,

that eternal candle
is the source of my shine
that eternal beauty
is behind my rhyme
without that candle
without that beauty
how could i
ever have
my share in life
101

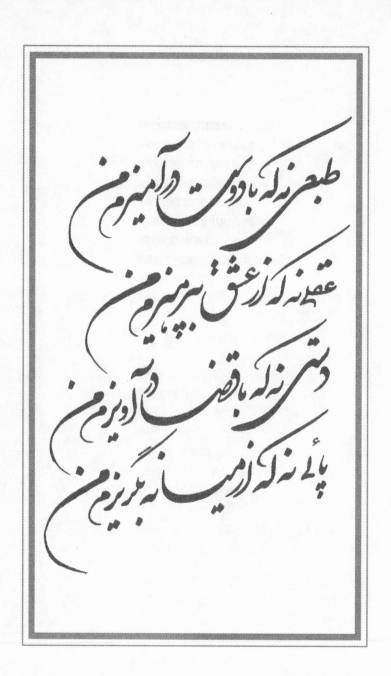

طبعی نه که با دوست در آمیزم من
عقلی نه که از عشق بپرهیزم من
دستی نه که با قضا در آویزم من
پایی نه که از میانه بگریزم من

i can't get together
with the beloved
i have no wisdom
to avoid love
i have no hands
to fight my fate
i have no legs
to run away very far
102

without looking at you
i can not touch the wine
without your hand
i can not win the dice
you are asking me
to dance from afar
without your music
dance will not arrive
103

i am in love with love
love is in love with me
my body fell in love
with my soul
and my soul fell in love
with me
we take turns in loving
we take turns in being loved
104

happiness is to reach
the next post every day
like flowing water
free from stillness
and melancholy
yesterday is gone and
took away its tale
today we must live
a fresh story again
105

Rumi,

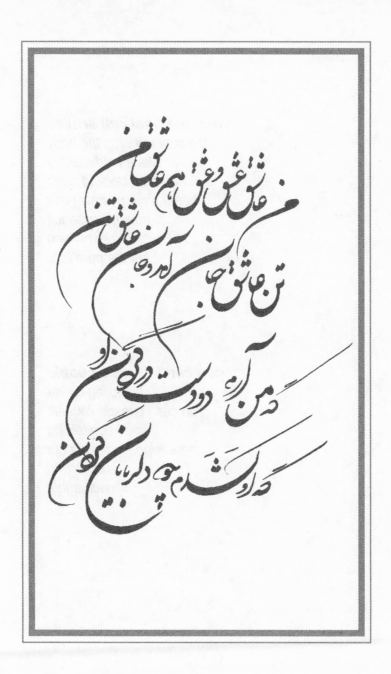

when the final call arrives
the soul will drop the body
like an old laundry
giving it back to earth
then molding a new body
from it's essence
which was nothing
but the pure light
106

you can't escape people
by acting clever
you can't escape yourself
if you keep talking
there is only one way out
silence and
silence again
107

Rumi,

if you don't keep the company
of those who live with love
hardship will strike
and you'll fall ill
be like a shadow chasing
the lovers of this world then
like the sun and moon
you'll give and receive
plenty of light
108

even if i resign
in an abbey
you'll get me drunk
even if i sit
in the house of Mecca
you'll make me worship an idol
i'll let go and
leave myself in your hands
since i can never know
what you have in mind
109

you'll arrive to
the eager hearts
but arrive very late
and when you arrive
like a short breath
that's all you stay
one day you come as a fawn
one day vicious like a lion
like a sword you appear
smooth and soft but
ready to cut
110

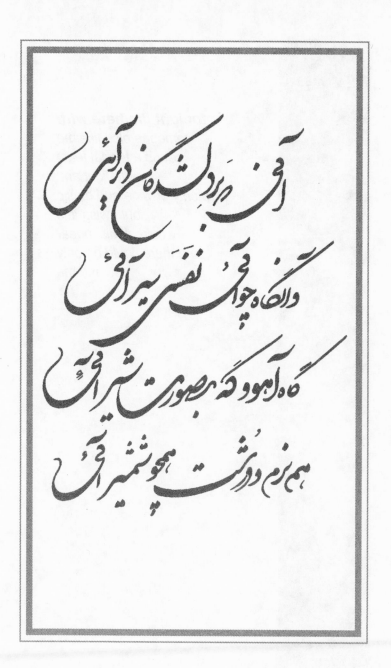

آفتاب برآ دلشدگان در آئی
وانگاه چو یک نفسی بر آئی

گاه آمده که به صورت شیرازی
هم نزم و درشت همچو شمشیر آئی

tonight i'm here with
someone else like me
set up a formal feast
candle light and
plenty of wine and music
but i wish this
would all disappear
and there could be only
you and me
111

Rumi,

i asked my mentor
in our happy hours
the ins and outs of this life
and far beyond
he said
your salvation is on the way
when you try to take
people's pain away

112

Dancing the Flame

love is
a great suspended sea
full of old secrets
full of sinking souls
only a drop
holding a bit of hope
and the rest
nothing but fears
113

love is
what makes people happy
love is
what justifies our being
i was given birth by
the mother
who is called love
to that mother i bestow
a hundred blessings
a hundred cheers
114

Rumi,

love is
best when many
sufferings arise from it
the one who avoids pain
can't know love
a hero is one
who in the journey of love
surrenders his life
with no qualms

115

love is
from the start to eternity
and the seekers of love
are countless forever
and tomorrow
on the day of judgement
any heart who is empty of love
will surely fail to pass

116

__love is__
the alchemy of the rising sun
a hundred thousand
lightnings in a cloud
and within me
the majesty of love
spreads a sea
drowning all the
galaxies above
117

__love is__
a mirror
you see nothing
but your reflection
you see nothing
but your real face
118

__Rumi,__

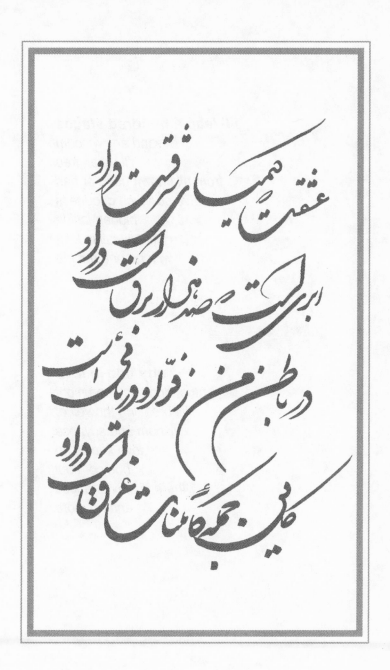

Dancing the Flame

i'll leap a hundred stages
beyond any wisdom
i'll break free
from all known good or bad
i have so much goodness
hidden inside
i'll finally fall in love
with no one but me
119

any one in love
must drink day and night
till breaking the veil of
wisdom and shyness
love knows no
body or soul
there is only oneness
and no more
120

Rumi,

any one in love
will have no religion
in the religion of love
there is no heresy or faith
love knows no
body heart or soul
there is only
oneness and no more
121

your lover may seem timid
what can he do
sleepless
going around your home
what can he do
when he kisses a lock of your hair
don't get mad
if a madman doesn't try
to break the chain
what can he do
122

all those in love are ready
to lose both worlds
in one stroke
let go of a
hundred years of life
in one day
travel a thousand miles
to experience a moment
and lose a thousand lives
for the sake of one heart
1.23

tomorrow when
men and women
resurrect with fear
of their account
i will show your love
in the palm of my hand
asking them to
deduct everything
from this single account
1.24

Rumi,

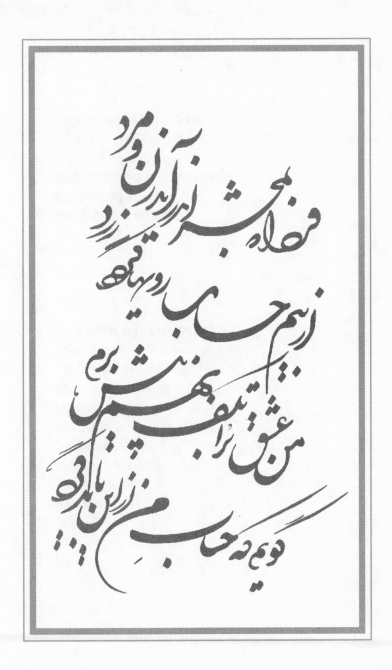

Dancing the Flame

come on messenger
don't hide the good news
even if you hang a
prison sign on a garden door
a garden will
not change to a jail

125

fallen in love with you
i will take no advice
i have tasted the poison
what good can sugar do
they say he is mad
and in chains
he must be put
mad is my heart
what is a chain
on my foot

126

Rumi,

in the journey of love
a thousand hearts and souls
will not suffice
only a traveller
ready to give a hundred lives
in every step
and not look back
can take this path
127

now and then
i hide or show up
now and then
i am moslem jew or christian
till my heart becomes
part of every heart
i will appear every day
with a different face
128

i am happy with a wine
that has no cup
i shine every morning
and enjoy myself every night
they say you will
end up with nothing
i am happy
with no end at all
129

i am happy with
no clothes or money
i am comfortable
when in pain
since i have surrendered
i am happy forever
not half happy
as you are
130

Rumi,

since i have learned
to love you
i've closed my eyes
to everyone
every flame
that love strikes
first catches on me
since i've been
scorched before

131

don't run away from me
i'm here to buy you
take a look at me
i'm the light
eager to find you
join me in my work
i'll prosper yours
don't be fed up with me
what i'm selling
is all yours

132

من پرسیدم تو پریانه شدم

از بانگ نی معشوقه چو کام شدم

نفسی سخنه شدم جام شدم

در هر قدمی دانه شدم دام شدم

i am the whole sea
not merely a drop
i am not cross eyed with
prejudice and pride
i express my existence
and every speck of me
cries aloud that
i am not just a particle
133

if you see me getting old
it's not from the
passing of time
my beloved being
coy and selfish
in every breath
i get cooked
i get raw
over and over
in every step
i'm used as a bait
or a trap
over and over
134

i wouldn't exchange
a bit of you
for the heavens above
i wouldn't exchange
the pain of your love
for both worlds
i've sacrificed my own
image in this world
i wouldn't exchange yours
for Adam's and more

135

no way i'll let anyone
take away this pain
no way i would
lose this love till i die
this gift of pain
given by my beloved
i won't exchange for all
the healing in the world

136

Rumi,

until last night
i used to complain
calling our separation unfair
i used to be in rage with
this unjust universe
but when i saw you
as only a part of me
with that vision i went
soundly to sleep

137

i am ready to bow
to you my beloved
since today i'm more
intoxicated than you are
i'm ready to swear on this
but why swear
if you can't believe me
i'd rather have more wine

138

i'm not fulfilled
but i don't want to see
anyone else who is
without touching
the earth at your gate
i don't desire
even the water of life
i have total faith in you
i'm ready to
let go of my life
i am ready to
let go of all other faiths

139

Rumi,

i know the habits
of my sweetheart
i am the oil and
the beloved's soul is fire
the tenderness of my soul
is from the light
my beloved beams
the darkness around
my sweetheart
is from the smoke
that i spread

140

Dancing the Flame

i'm so in love with your face
what do you think i should do
i'm shy to look at
your happy eyes
what do you think i should do
every moment
the pang of love
makes me scream
for God's sake
what do you think i should do
141

your super perfection
teaches me how to love
i get my love poems and odes
by simply looking at you
my love poems and odes arrive
your dancing image
playing alive
on my heart's stage
that's the source
of my own happy dances
142

Rumi,

your love is
in place of religion
and faith for me
as long as i live
i don't want to learn
patience in love
i thought to leave you alone
for a few days
i simply couldn't
why pretend it now
143

i can't choose anyone but you
what can i do
i have no medicine
for this distressed heart
what can i do
you ask me how long
am i going to spin
i have nothing else to do
what can i do
144

i'm a spinner in dance
i want a musician
who spins with me
i want a Venus
twisting like Saturn
i am the life
seeking the essence
of the soul
i am not a sad bird
in ruins like an owl
145

i am the one with hunger
but have the happiness of
the one fulfilled
i am a fox who is
filled with lions
i have a self within
fearful of unknown dreams
but don't look at my fears
'n essence i'm a brave soul
146

Rumi,

i have become
the owner of a land
with no time and place
i have become the mystic
of a treasure
filled with gold
with a heart burning
in the mother of pearl
i have become
a sea of gracing souls
147

i'm your flute
i only drink
from your lips
unless you play me
i have no sound
of my own
if you see me silent
i'm treasuring
your sweetness within
148

i used to be wise and clever
just like you
i used to brush aside
all the claims of
the existence of love
now that i'm lost
crazy and carefree
it seems i've been
living this way
all along
149

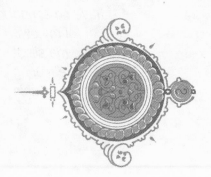

Rumi,

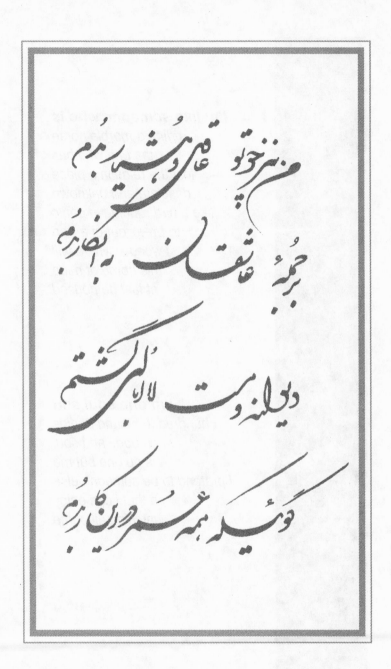

من نیز خود تو قلبی دلشیاربرم

برجمه عاشقان به انتظاربرم

دیلنه دوست لاابالی گشتم

گوئیکه همه عشم دلان کاربرم

i'm like someone who is
riding a marble horse
the one who has
lost the reins in a place
desolate and unknown
like a bird running in panic
to break out of a trap
i wonder where will
this horse of mine
at last be housed
150

i'm one soul and
a hundred thousand bodies
each body and soul
is no one but me
i pretend to be someone else
so that i can enjoy
watching all of me
151

Rumi,

the moon is rising
yet i'm going down
my beloved is sobering up
while i'm going drunk
my dear God whatever you
reckon from now on
don't call it life
since i am gone
152

the drum begs for
the drummer's beat
with every strike saying
i'll tell a new tale
if you beat me
with mercy or rage
like all lovers
i'll be happy
to tell my tale
153

for a while we went to
a teacher as a child
for a while we were
happy among friends
listen to our story
how it ends
we arrived as clouds
and were swept away
by winds
154

try your best in this life
that is the best you can do
when your entire life hangs
on one last breath
it is obvious
there's not much
you can do
155

hide my secrets
within your soul
keep my world
hidden from your world
if your spirit lets you
wrap my spirit
with yours
make this heresy of mine
the guiding light for yours

156

life without you is a waste
how can it be named life
if you're not there
i swear a life without you
will not be called anything
but death

157

my dear heart
please cope with me
in this event
my dear soul
please go along now
but my patience
run along since
you can't stand the grief
and my poor logic
you're only a child
so go out and play
158

you're crawling in a corner
pulling away from the crowd
crying from heavenly troubles
and tired of bitter smiles
if you're a lion
why run away from lions
if you're a vulture
go to find your own kind
159

Rumi,

clear your heart from
jealousy greed and grudge
uproot your bad habits
and bad thoughts
let go of denial
it causes your loss
welcome confession and
your profit will rise
160

if you're happy
even for a moment
with your sweetheart
seize the moment
as the fulfillment
of your life
beware
let no breath
go to waste
since you will not find
that breath again
161

if you desire to see
eternal life
or discover wealth
in poverty
don't follow your path timidly
to discover real life
enter it like a hero

162

it is a waste to play
tambourine to the deaf
or lock up a beauty idol
in the house of the blind
it is a waste to push honey
into lips quivering with fever
or force the marriage
of a gay man with a beauty queen

163

Rumi,

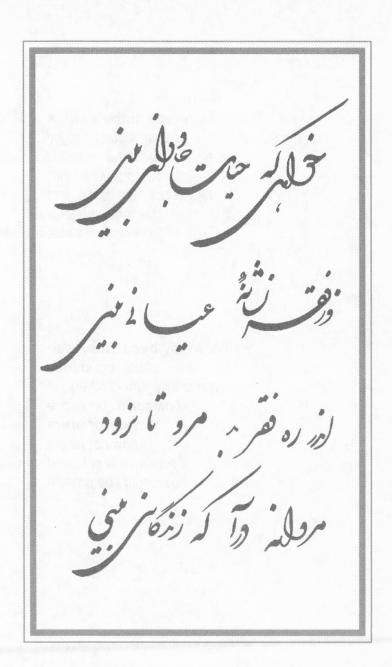

خامشی که حیات جاودانی منی
ورقه نشهٔ عیانی منی
از ره فقر مرو تا نرود
مرحله درآ که زندگانی منی

Dancing the Flame

be happy since a sufi's
foundation is on joy
a sufi is fulfilled from within
having a pure heart
he will not experience grief
he is the emperor
of the kingdom inside
164

you're in my eyes otherwise
how could i see
you're in my mind otherwise
how could i be in love
yonder where
i know not where
if your love is not there
how could i be present
165

Rumi,

under all these love poems
and lamentations
there is pain and fire
although love affairs
can cause happiness
where is the happiness
encouraged by the beloved
166

how long
will you worry
about making a living
how long
will you pamper your body
stuff your mouth
throat and belly
how long
should you bust
your jaws and teeth
worry about
your soul for a moment
167

you can never breathe
healing to your body
till you cut off
worries from your breath
though you're weary at times
surely you can pull through
168

this heart will one day
find you a sweetheart
this soul will one day
take you to the beloved
seize your pain as a blessing
your pain will one day
lead you to healing
169

Rumi,

i haven't lost hope
even if you've left me
or if you chose
someone else
i long for you
as long as i live
since there is lots of
hope in every despair

170

if you fall behind your beloved
you'll recede
every branch fallen
from a tree will rot
when you dwell
in someone's heart
you'll be like the
pupil of their eyes

171

i'm not really me
but if for one moment i were
i would scatter this world
like specs of dust
if i were me
with a departed heart
i would uproot myself
like a tree
172

you're like a flower
born from the
essence of laughter
good fortune and happiness
you're free and luscious
like a blossoming branch
173

Rumi,

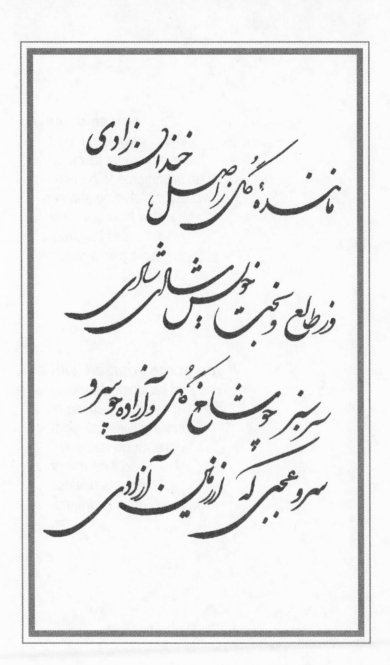

ماند ه گانی زاصل خدای زادی

ور طلع و نجبت و نبیل خوبیش شاهی شاهی

سر سبز چو شاخ گی و آزاده چو سرو

سرو عجبی که از زمین آزادی

you said i'm
irresponsible and mad
i say you must be crazy
expecting me to be wise
you said i have no shame
with a face like steel
yes but steel
acting as a mirror
174

if you gorge yourself with
wine and kabob and candies
you'll fall asleep dreaming of
drinking water all night
once awakened you'll
still be thirsty
water is useless
when you drink in dreams
175

Rumi,

even if life is
a desolate desert
with no sign posts
never lose hope
in the paradise
of your soul
sweet dates can grow
from dead oaks
176

if for the span of one breath
you're allowed a glimpse
of life's secret
you'll let go of
everything at once
but as long as you're
intoxicated with yourself
forever you're fuzzy
fall for the beloved
to be aware and clear
177

if you're hunted by God
you're set free
from all worries
if you've fallen for yourself
you're trapped
know that you are
your own curtain
don't sit behind yourself
too long
you'll get tired and bored
178

Rumi,

if i only knew
my own value
and perfection
i would pull out
of this lowly earth
evacuate myself
and rise to
soar my soul
to the ninth heaven
179

Dancing the Flame

i saw unhappiness
very depressed
selling a barrel of pain
in the market place
what is happening
i asked
you're selling happiness
he said
putting me out of business
180

you haven't experienced
heresy
how can you be talking of
faith
you haven't let go of
yourself
how can you talk about the
beloved
you're so busy tending
your lusts
how can you talk about
the soul
181

Rumi,

the world is luscious green
everywhere smiling gardens
manifesting the face
of the beloved
in every path diamonds are
shining showing the source
in every direction
souls connecting with souls

182

the other day
a tender voiced nightingale
sitting by a stream
was singing this song
you can make a flower
out of emerald ruby
cumin and gold
but it will have no
aroma of it's own

183

you're not earth
you're not water
you're something else
you're journeying beyond
the water and earth
body is a stream
soul is the water of life
but you're in a place
beyond this or that
184

Rumi,

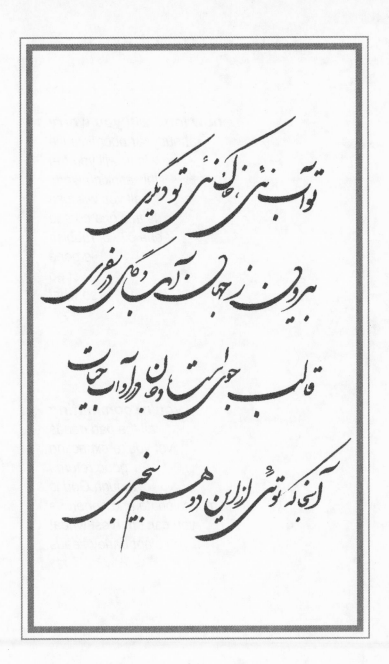

تو آب نئی، کِنئی تو دیگری

برون ز جهت آب و کای دیگری

قالب جوئی است و در آداب حیات

آنکه توئی از این دو هم سخیری

how long will you worry
about your poor little life
how long will you fret
this stinking world
all you will lose
is this one corpse
if one pile of rubbish
is gone
let go
so what

185

you're committing
all the bad deeds
yet you're expecting
good returns
though God is
compassionate and generous
you can't harvest wheat
if you plant barley seeds

186

Rumi,

like a feather
sticking together
with your friends
you can fly as wings
and as long as you fly
you rule over the wind
but cut away
as a single feather
you're not only useless
you're gone with the wind

187

make sure you won't regret
whatever you've done before
like a sufi never mention
the yesterdays
you belong to the moment
make sure you
won't lose this one breath

188

enter this garden
carrying flowers
if you're not all thorns
show your harmony
if you're not a stranger
don't show a poisonous face
if you're not a snake
read this impression
if you're not engraved
yourself on the wall
189

if you're with everyone
since you're without me
you're with no one
if you're with no one
when you're with me
you're with all
don't be trapped by everyone
be everyone on your own
when you're the laughing stock
you're on the top
190

Rumi,

your home is
on top of the world
yet you see yourself
as low as the ground
carving your image
only in the earth
while you've left
your real self behind
191

one day this blooming bough
will bear fruits
one day this falcon of quest
will bring a hunt
your beloved's dream
appears and disappears
but how long
before it lasts
at last
192

if you seek this world
you are a mercenary
if you seek paradise
you've lost the truth
if you're happy and carefree
you're excused
since you have never known
ᵗʰe happiness in love's agony
193

my dear heart you really
never followed God
you never regretted
your wrong doings
you became mystic
and religious
pious and wise
you became everything
but never a moslem
to yield it all
194

Rumi,

my dear friend
don't expect me
to sustain for you
in grief
don't expect anything
from me but happiness
intoxication and good times
since God created us
only for this
i wreck logic and
fight a sober mind
195

in every heart there is
a ray of your compassion
on every altar
there is a shedding of tears
one everlasting night
one glorious moonlight
i'll open to you the doors
to my longings
so far hidden in my heart
196

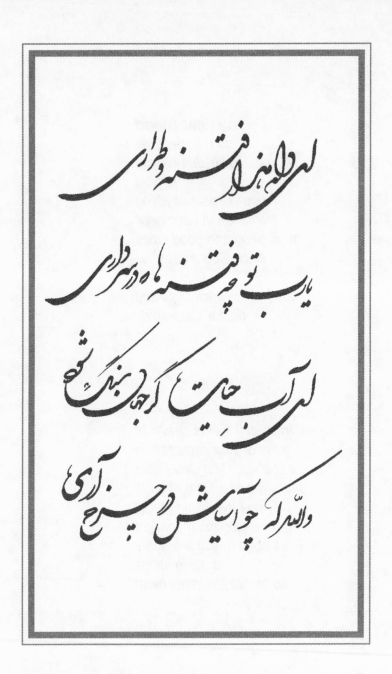

لئی دام نهاد فتنه طرّاری

یا رب تو چه فتنه‌ها در بهر داری

لئی آب حیات گر چه بنیادِ شمع

والله که چو آتش در حسـرت آری

Rumi,

my God you are a trap
*of a thousand
conspiracies and tricks
my God you've many
mischievous plans
hidden in your head
if the whole world
becomes one stone
i swear to you
my water of life
you will turn it
like a mill stone*

197

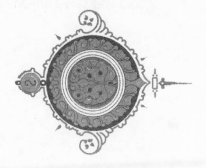

your imagination my friend
fills you with lots of wind
for no reason
you become happy or sour
i saw you in fire today
and let you be
till you cook to become
a clever and wise master
198

if you really knew
who was in charge
you would wipe out
ego from your heart
if you really had an insight
not for a moment
would you serve anyone else
199

Rumi,

the cry of the viol's music
filled with flame
uproar and temptation
the messenger of the desert
the exposer of the
hidden secrets of the heart
where are you coming from
200

you'll be smart and alert
when you eat less
you'll feel stupid and lazy
when you're stuffed
you'll be miserable when
you fill your miserable self
you won't feel slighted
when you're lighted
201

Dancing the Flame

you have no eyes to see
the one who gives you
life and death
the one who makes you
laugh or depressed
that one is everywhere
from your toe to head

202

if you won't fall in love
go spin your wool
hundreds of busy works
and changes of color
if your skull is empty
of the wine of love
you might as well
lick the bowl
of those who do

203

Rumi,

whatever may happen
don't be afraid
come what may
since it won't stay
don't be afraid
savor the moment
and leave what is gone
and fear not
for what may come
204

anyone who has
enough to eat
and a nest to rest
tell him to be happy
the world is his
since he's in need of no one
and no one is
in need of him
205

i've vanished in God
and God is mine
search for God
nowhere else but in my soul
if i tell you i have a king
i'm misleading you
since i am the king
206

i have a tongue
beside this tongue
i have a hell and paradise
beside the ones you know
free spirited humans are
alive in others' souls
their pure diamond
is from another source
207

Rumi,

love arrived and
like blood
filled my skin and veins
emptied me out and
re-filled with my friend
my beloved has taken over
every part of me
nothing is left of me
but an empty name
208

many are sad and never know
where the sorrow comes from
many are happy but ignorant
that it is all from God
many go right and left
not knowing where to go
many me and us are
going on within
but remain unknown
209

Dancing the Flame

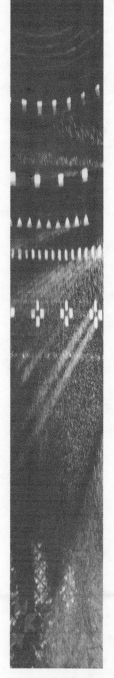

if there is no fire
in the heart
then what is this smoke
if it isn't incense burning
then what is this aroma
why me falling in love
and vanishing away
why a candle moth burning
yet happy in flame
210

all my life
my soul's been without me
yet infamous among
female and male
leaving this life and
this world is easy
the difficulty is
bidding you farewell
211

Rumi,

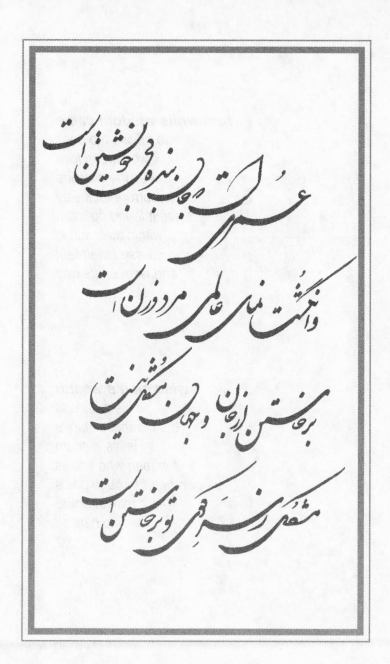

عشق است جان بندهٔ خویشتن است

وانگشت نمای عالمی مردوزان است

برخاستن از جان و جهان مشکی نیست

مشکل رخ کی تو برخیستن است

Dancing the Flame

for awhile wisdom came
to advise the ones
who are in love
it sat by the wayside
to corrupt their way
since it found no room
within their minds
it kissed their feet
and went on its way

212

a wise man's wealth
is his madness
the madness in love
is his wisdom
the man who knows
his own heart through pains
is a total stranger
to himself

213

make your journeys
at night
since the night will lead you
to many secrets
and hide you
from your enemies
at night hearts are loving
and eyes sleepy
all night long
we're busy
with no one
but the sweetheart
214

anyone who is not in love
cannot be as light as a soul
like moon and stars
cannot be orbiting restlessly
hear it from me
as the final word
a flag can never dance
with no air and no wind
215

there is a passage connecting
our tongue and heart
sustaining the secrets
of the world and soul
as long as our tongue is locked
the channel is open
the moment our tongue unlocks
the passage will close

216

my dear heart
there is a path
through the soul
to the beloved
there is a hidden way
from a confused mind
to the sweetheart
even if the six directions
in your life are closed
have no fear
there is a passage
from the depth of your existence
to the highest love

217

Rumi,

the mystery hidden
in my friend's words
i shall not reveal
those are the
precious pearls
i shall not pierce
i fear to utter words
while i am asleep
for that fear
during the nights
i shall not sleep

218

i've drunk from the wine
whose chalice is the soul
i'm drunk for the one
who enslaved my mind
a candle has arrived
and set me on fire
a candle in whose orbit
turns the mighty sun

219

i have gone crazy
that's why i can't sleep
how can a madman
find a pasture to rest
since God is needless
and never sleepy
any one mad about God
will surely keep
away from sleep
220

why am i sad and dark
like a bat
am i blind or has grief
targeted me as one
i'm in seventh heaven
though on earth my picture is
reflected in water and clay
but who ever steals
a star from water
221

when those who
are in love meet
they meet
in a different world
the intoxication of
the wine of love
they seek
is a different ecstasy
the lessons we learn in school
have nothing to do with
the lessons we learn in love

222

whatever happens in
the tangible or unknown
whatever happens
be it good or bad
is ordered by God
in fate and destiny
i keep trying but
my fate keeps telling me
something is going on
that is out of your hand

223

Dancing the Flame

in the journey of quest
the wise and the madman
are the same
in the path of love
the kin and the stranger
are the same
anyone who's been given
the blessings of eternal wine
in his religion
Mecca and the shrine of idols
are the same

224

as long as i have
the vision of the beloved
even if i'm in the shrine of idols
it's a mistake to leave that
and go to Mecca
with the beloved's vision
any temple is my Mecca
and without that
Mecca is filled
with idols of heresy

225

Rumi,

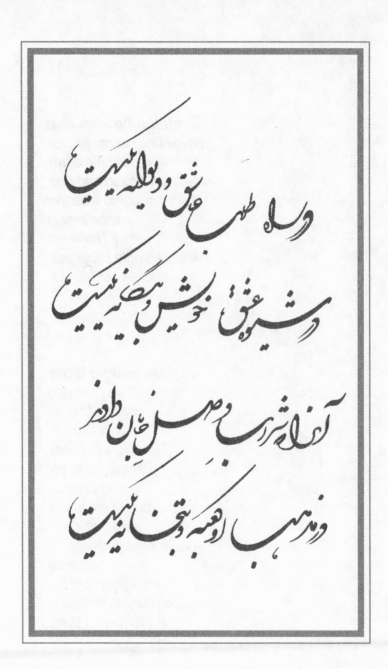

all the flowers and
graceful trees in my garden
only remind me of my
sweetheart's torso and face
i swear to whoever
you believe in
today i have not
even a single sober vein
226

why are you so bitter
aren't you carrying
loads of honey
or are you
loaded with honey
but have no buyer
or is it that
you are incapable
and that's why
you seem confused
or maybe
you're capable but
everything is worthless
in this market place
227

Rumi,

you're fulfilled
i'm not
so what's the cure
if there's no love
what's the other choice
you said if i show patience
i'll be rewarded with faith
you're the believer of faith
tell me
without the beloved
what is a faith
228

when my pain
causes my healing
my lows transform to highs
and heresy became faith
my soul and heart and body
were blocking my journey before
but now my body became heart
heart became soul
and the soul turned
to be the creator
229

to keep you ignorant of
how conscious the earth is
just like a rabbit
closed eyed yet awake
earth keeps foaming
like a pot
a thousand times
to hide its boiling core
230

out of this world and our lives
there is someone
who is nursing us
the one whom we
can never comprehend
i only know this much
we are the shadow
of this one
and the world is
the shadow of us
231

Rumi,

there is a world
beyond the world of
heresy and faith
the place where not
everyone raw and vain can go
the one who desires to dwell
in such a world
must sacrifice the soul
and give the heart in thanks
for the blessed soul
232

look for the world
surfing the blood
in my veins
the magic and the magician
dwell together
in my veins
who cares if
the traces of madness
are found there
how can blood rest
when it runs through
veins like my veins
233

Dancing the Flame

from the start
i've had a different pact
with eternity
this life of corpses
are separate territories
my dear clergy
you're so proud of
your midnight prayers
there is another dimension
beyond those prayers

234

when your friend
seeks the company
of your enemy too long
that friend must be
left behind
leave alone honey
mixed with poison
run away from the fly
that nests on a snake

235

Rumi,

you're so stuck
with this short lived life
no one can talk to you
anymore of death
your soul is yearning to arrive
and the home is death
yet your ride
has gone to sleep
somewhere midway

236

the pal within you
the one who gives you breath
will also give hope
to reach your final quest
up to your last moment
take every breath
from the one inside
who is not playing with you
but generously
endows your every breath

237

the one you know me
as me it isn't me
who do you think it is
i utter no words
with my tongue
who do you think it is
i'm only a shirt
from my head to my toes
the one whose shirt is me
who do you think it is

238

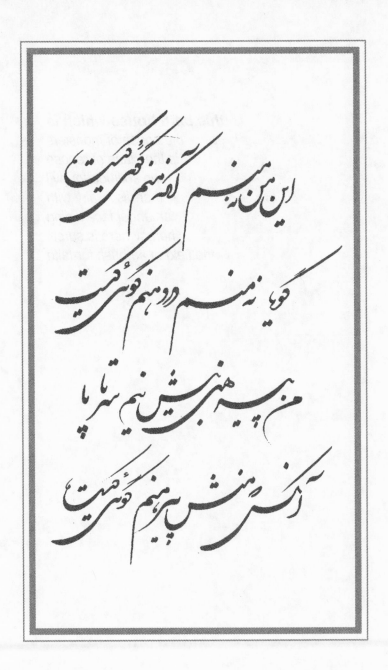

Dancing the Flame

this bath house which is
the house of monsters
is the place of repose
and solitude for evil
there is a fairy with
an angel face hiding
heresy here is surely
the field of ambush for faith

239

Rumi,

this ceramic form
my body
is merely the chalice
of my heart
this wisdom in my thoughts
is the brewing wine
of my heart
all these seeds of knowledge
are nothing but bait
for my heart
and even what i'm
telling you now
is spoken by me
yet it's only a message
from my heart

240

this flaring chest of mine
is filled
with my beloved's teachings
and today that i've fallen ill
is nothing but a fever of love
i'll be glad to avoid
anything my doctor orders
except of course
for honey and wine
offered by my beloved's lips

241

this spring you own
is not the one everyone seeks
not every water wheel
goes around by your stream
not everyone can draw
a far shooting bow
is not everyone's challenge
it takes a hero
not every meager
man can do

242

Rumi,

who owns all these wines
which have no grail
who set this trap
while we caught the bird
who owns all this
delicious honey
pistachio and almond
and pours it constantly
on every one
who falls in love
243

this cosmos and
these galaxies that are
the limits of our vision
is less than a cane
held by God's hand
if every speck of dust
and drop of water
changes to a giant whale
they will be merely a
single fish in this vast sea
244

this whirling cosmos
is at the service of
our whimsical wish
this existence is the source
of our non-existence
behind all these curtains
there is someone
who is nursing us
we haven't been born yet
what you see
is merely our shadow

245

Rumi,

i say to the night
if you don't
see me intoxicated
or my sleeplessness
seems exaggerated
it's because my body
is short lived
in this lowly life
while my sleep
has flown away
like an angel
to the heavens
246

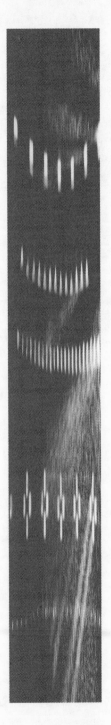

Dancing the Flame

you see no center
you're so ego ridden
within your shell
your senses are
the brain of your body
and your brain
the sense of your soul
remember
that there is a friend
within your soul
once you surpass
the body sense and soul
there is nothing but the friend
247

let's be fair
love brings nothing
but good deeds
if there are failings
it is caused by our evil nature
it may only be your lust
that you call love
there is a long journey
between the two
248

Rumi,

in my head
i've another dream
my true love
is an image of
another beloved
i swear to God even love
is not enough to satisfy me
after this autumn
i'll have another spring
249

in my heart
inside and out
is all beloved
in my body
blood and veins
is none but beloved
how can there be any
room for religion
or Godlessness in me
since my existence
is overflowing
with beloved
250

what type of day is this
with two shining suns
a day beyond and above
every day known
a whirling cosmos is endowing
and calling everyone on earth
good news to those in love
call today your own
251

anyone who thinks
heart is what is in the chest
takes only a few steps
and wants the reward to arrive
the prayer rug rosary virtue
confession and repentance
are none but the journey
while everyone
thinks he's already arrived
252

Rumi,

anyone who promises you
help in hard days
beware he only gives
you a free breath
in good times
the whole world
is your friend
but in depressing nights
there are few
with known address
253

the one who has
a pain but can express
right from the heart
shall rest at ease
but look at this
rare flower blossoming
right within me
i can describe
neither its color nor scent
254

what is it that
makes our face
shine with pleasure
what is it that when absent
darkens our face
for one moment it
disappears from the face
and in another
appears from an
unknown place
255

Rumi,

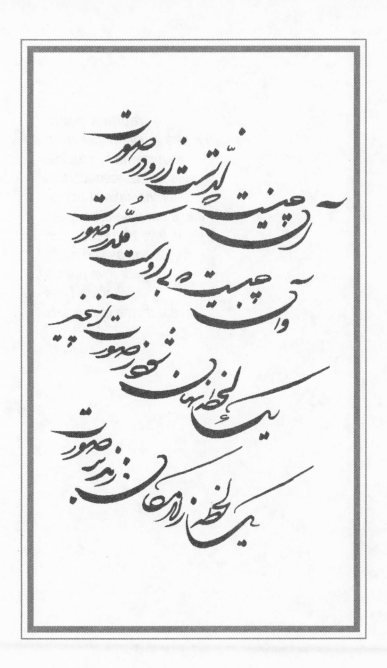

Dancing the Flame

recite a poem
but as a tender father say it
as a rhyme in couplets
put your wisdom
for the sake of advice
into the rhyme of couplets
in love and separation
and as you recite
your love poems
say a few lines
in the rhyme of couplets

256

Rumi,

we are the secret
treasures of God
we are the ocean
holding endless pearls
from the high moon
to the small fish
there is no one but us
sitting on a throne
and being the king
is no one but us

257

searching for love
once in a while
we feel at a loss
feeling the pain
of separation
once in a while
we sizzle in fire
once you and i
are cleansed from
the you and the me
only then you and i
without this us
will be happy
258

Rumi,

i thought if my lust
like a mad dog
would age
i could leash it
with repentance
but it will break
the leash
once it sees death
how else can i
manage this wild beast
259

what am i supposed to do
if my dark night
doesn't want to change
to a bright day
what am i supposed to do
if my luck
doesn't want to
give me a ride
what am i supposed to do
i said once fortune
comes my way
i'll buy up the whole world
but if fortune
gives me no chance
what am i supposed to do

_260_

Rumi,

there are two attitudes
rendering us useless
two bad manners
chaining us for good
one
intoxication in self glory
the other
awakening coming too late
261

we are the new farmers
in this ancient field
harvesting sadness
from happy seeds
like short lived tulips
in a doomed plain
no sooner arising from earth
we pledge ourselves into the winds
262

we set fire to our shops
jobs and trades
we chose to learn poetry
love songs and lyrics instead
in the journey of love
where love is our
soul and heart and eyes
we riveted all three
to love in turn

263

i break all the rules
in pains and healings
i break all the rules
in love and sufferings
you saw me repent
many times with pure heart
now watch me break
my repentances all

264

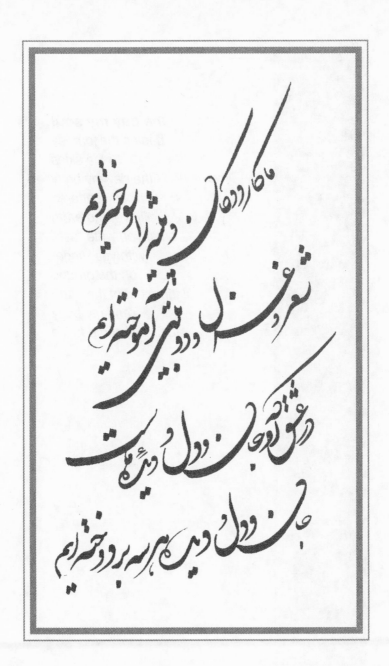

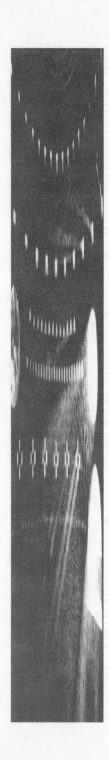

the day my soul
begins the journey
to the skies
is the day my body
has scattered
all over the earth
but if you write "rise"
with your finger
on the ground
i'll jump out of the earth
and my body
again will come to life

265

Rumi,

the day love
battles my heart
my soul will fly away
barefoot from here on
crazy will be the man
who thinks i'll be sober
wise will be the one
who'll avoid me
from there on
266

how can any heart
who sees the hidden beauty
be engrossed with
the material of this world
the heart will abandon the eyes
on the day of calling
if it ignores the eternal beauty
and busies itself
with its own soul
267

anyone who is happy
with what he has or
however he makes a living
sleeps or prays
will never lean
but on God
since he knows
the attention of the crowd
will be good for half an hour
and no more

268

Rumi,

anyone who is given
mind and knowledge
is set up for life
and easy living
but anyone whose head
is left with emptiness
it's been filled
with lots of belongings
269

don't look at a man
who is jack of all trades
look at his loyalty
to his promises
if a man gives and
keeps his word
he is above and beyond
all characters found
270

the one who
set me ablaze
in this world
also put a hundred
locks on my tongue
once i was engulfed
in the fire in
six directions
no sooner had i begun to sigh
a hand came down
on my mouth and
properly shut me up
271

Rumi,

what is the use of life
or wife or children
for any one who
has an insight into you
you bestow both worlds
to the one
you first drive insane
once insane what is
the use of
both worlds
to anyone
any more
27.2

who is the one
who sees the external
right from within
who is the one
who casts a hundred magic spells
when watching the insane in love
try your own eyes
see how they see
who is the one
who is looking out
through your eyes for you

273

i don't imagine
even our soul
is as close to us
as the one we love
i swear to God i never
try to remember my beloved
remembering is only
for those who are absent in us

274

Rumi,

my dear heart
you'll never lose
in love
how can you lose
your soul
while you become
the soul
in the beginning
you descended from
heavens to earth
and at the end
you'll ascend
from the earth to heaven

275

Dancing the Flame

remembrance of God and
a human rises to the absolute
see how splendour arrives
when God shines through
this miraculaous ocean
this human inner world
once set in motion
the cry of
"I AM GOD"
will rise and behold
276

now that you've stolen
the soul of the world
there is no use
sitting at home
the day you were
transformed to a moon
you had no idea
everyone would point
their finger at you
277

Rumi,

tonight the wine bearer
passed around the
musk like wine
then stole every heart
and penetrated every faith
pouring wine after wine
causing a storm to rise
unlinking forever
the chains of sanity

278

i wish much grief
for the heart of
any unloyal kind
i wish the vanishing
of any unfaithful friend
no one remembers me
in these times of sadness
except for sorrow
my admired loyal pal

279

in times of fasting
the earth of your body
changes to gold
like a stone that is
powdered for eye-liner
every bite you've eaten
becomes precious as pearls
every moment you've waited
will be diamonds in worth
280

you are the solution
to all my problems
your blessings intoxicate
blossoms and trees
and in the whole garden
every flower and thorn
are drunk with
your love potion
give me a chalice
by which all are
but one
281

you my peaceful pals
wandering around the world
why are you at a loss
searching for an idol
the one whom you're looking for
out in the world
if you search inside
you will find
you are the one
282

my dear heart
you can't find
your path with commotion
you can't reach
union without annihilation
once you're in the skies
where the beloved's
birds are flying
as long as you
struggle to fly
they will give you
no wings
283

my dear heart
keep your desires
tied to your foot
put your hope
in the one
who's guiding you
when you see
none of your
wishes have come true
don't lose hope
chain your heart
to no one but God

284

rise o day
the particles desire dancing
to the one
the air and the cosmos
are dancing
happy souls
with no head or feet
will be dancing
and i'll whisper
in your ear
where the dance
will take place
285

o love
they think of you
as an angel
or as a human
or above and beyond
the Solomon's seal
they think of you
as the soul's dwelling
in the universe's mold
but i live with you
as no one ever knows
286

Dancing the Flame

this being alone
is worth more than
a thousand lives around
this freedom
is worth more than
all the estates in the world
to be in solitude
with God
is more precious than
life or belongings
or whatever you've had

287

Rumi,

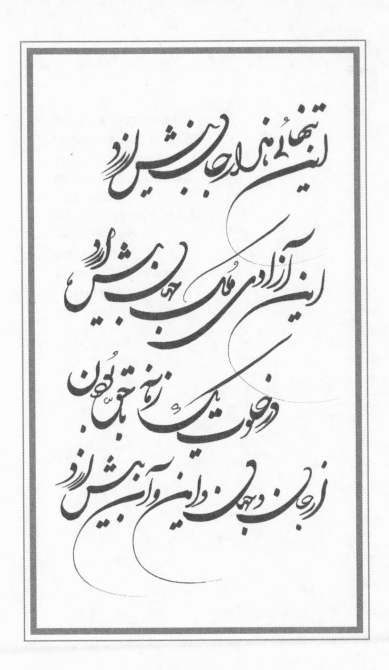

this human feature
designed and composed
is an impression
tied to this grief ridden
animal stall
now a monster
now an angel
now being wild
who knows what talisman
is this bundle
so tightly tied

288

this love is heading to
where the brave are
this bold deer moves
into the lion's den
this house of love
has flourished with
hopes and dreams
do you imagine
it will fall apart
without you
289

if you take this
incident very hard
by your meek struggle
no solution will arrive
you need a key
made of God's blessing
to open and
undo the lock
290

be kind to the human
who can't go to sleep
be kind to the one
who is thirsty
and has no water
be kind since any one
who has no generosity
has no reward
in God's presence

291

smile at every human
and you're doing
a pious deed and
you'll get back
a sweet smile
in return
i'm pouring tears
so that you can have wine
i'm burning my heart
so that you'll have kabob

292

Rumi,

__i asked a person__
with knowledge of
logic and proofs
who is the one
whose knowledge of life
is the truth
he gently hinted to me
you tender soul
this is the language of the birds
only Solomon the prophet knows

293

i was a pious preacher
you changed me to a poet
and in me you instilled
rebel rousing and
drunkenness in every feast
i was a solemn
man of sustained prayer
you made me the playing object
of street children

294

listen if you can
bear listening
joining the beloved
is to cut off
from oneself
keep silence where
visions are expressed
since the words of knowers
are all about seeing

295

Rumi,

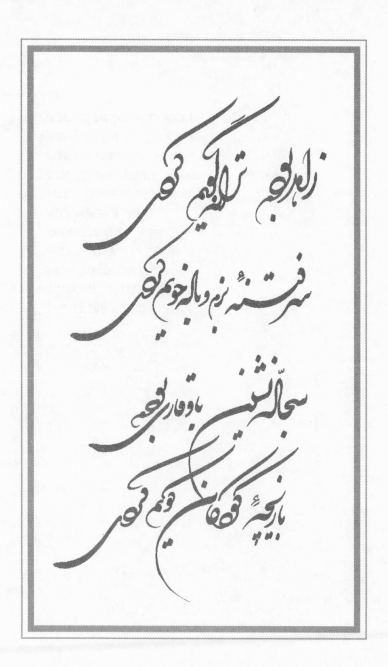

Dancing the Flame

i cannot be at peace
my beloved
without you
i cannot recount
your benevolences
even if every hair
on my body changes
to a tongue
i cannot express
your blessings
a thousand in one

296

Rumi,

without love
partying and good times
won't go very far
without love
human existence
won't elate and evolve
if a hundred drops of rain
fall from the clouds
over the sea
without the motion
of love
not one drop
can create a hidden
precious pearl

297

i wish you happiness
and your lips full of smiles
i wish you'd bring
joyous moments
to soul and hearts
of everyone in love
and if anyone sees you
but shows no smile
i wish he'd live like a black pen
dark and confused in life
298

whoever passes
by my grave
will become entranced
and if he stands in wait
will eternally go drunk
if he goes to the sea
the sea will ebb and flow
in ecstasy
and if he walks on the land
graves and tombstones
will be enraptured
299

Rumi,

come back my beloved
see how desperately
i need you
come back and see
my long sleepless nights
but then how wrong
how wrong to think
this separation will
spare my life
till you see me
once more
300

this isn't a real dance
when you can leap
at any moment
and rise painlessly
like a speck of dust
real dance is when you
rise above both worlds
tear your heart away
and are ready to let go
of your life
301

come
whoever you are
come
come again
even if you are godless
and a worshipper of
fire and idols
come
our home is the home of
never losing hope
come
even if you break
your repentance vows
a hundred times
come again
come

Rumi Shrine, Konya   302

Rumi,

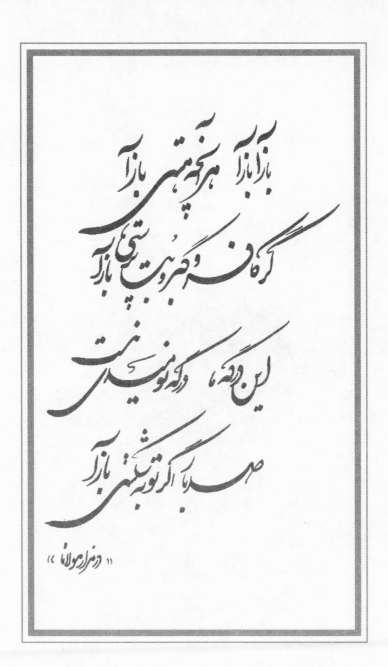

بازا بازآ هرآنچه هستی بازآ
گر کافر و گبر و بت پرستی بازآ
این درگه ما درگه نومیدی نیست
صد بار اگر توبه شکستی بازآ

« دز مزار مولانا »

Dancing the Flame

225

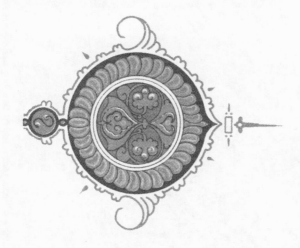

Rumi,

RUMI

Jalaloddin Mohammed Balkhi Rumi, was a solemn, pious man in the 13th century small town of Konya located in Turkey today. He was born in September 1207 in the city of Balkh, today's Afghanistan, then a city in Khorasan province, part of the Persian empire (Iran today). As a child he had fled with his family from their home town of Balkh, before the invading Monguls arrived. It took many years and thousands of miles before they settled in this quiet town. By the time he was 30 years of age he was speaking Persian, Arabic, Turkish, and knew all types of knowledge of the day including the exoteric sciences. He was a very respected preacher and scholar of Islamic philosophy, logic, and divine law. Life was smooth sailing, and he was basking in popularity,

a candle
spreading light
a Mecca
gathering the crowd

Then, close to forty years old, a fire, a thunderstorm bundled as a man named Shams, hits him very hard and sets him aflame. Their relationship has become known as a friendship, a pure love full of mysteries, and perhaps the zenith of spiritual connectedness ever known between two men.

Shams, an unknown man of about sixty, from the far away town of Tabriz to the east, with the specific mission of meeting Rumi arrives in Konya, and on a special day goes to Rumi's library, or grabs the reigns of the mule Rumi is riding and stops him in the middle of the road amidst his followers. Legends of their first encounter is still speculated upon as new scenarios unfold from his poems and stories. But all agree that from the moment of meeting Shams, Rumi was not the same man any more. Rumi himself puts it best,

> *I was a pious preacher*
> *you changed me to a poet*
> *and in me you instilled*
> *rebel rousing and*
> *drunkenness in every feast*
> *i was a solemn*
> *man of sustained prayer*
> *you made me the playing object*
> *of street children*

In the following months, Rumi and Shams meet for long hours of conversation, day and night, and Rumi abandons his pulpit, robe, and followers. He gambles everything in an intense mystic love,

> *blessed is the gambler*
> *who has lost everything*
> *except the desire*
> *to gamble*
> *once more*

Rumi,

In the following years, now together with Shams, now forced to separate with longings, Rumi, who had always despised poetry, overflows with 65,000 verses of poems; to many, the greatest in music, rhyme, and mystic meanings in the Persian language, surpassing every poet before and after to the present time.

> *i was dead*
> *i came alive*
> *i was tears*
> *i became laughter*
> *all because of love*

And in spite of all his previous religious teaching he begins dancing the flame, leaping in jubilation in his own created dynamic dance of whirling dervishes, with drunkenness triggered at times by a simple word, or by the sound of hammering in the market place.

> *i don't really need wine*
> *to get drunk*
> *i don't really need music*
> *to feel delight*
> *without a wine pal*
> *music and dance*
> *I'm intoxicated*
> *happy and gone*

The Life of Rumi* is celebrated on all continents and in all languages. He sees himself not belonging to any land, culture, or religion, He

has created the saintliest and wisest book in the
Mathnavi (25,000 verses) and the most rebellious
in the *Divan e Shams e Tabrizi (40,000* verses),
both books written down by his students as he
recited them. These books take the spiritual
experience with God, with friend, beloved,
sweetheart, to unimaginable levels.

> *come inside the fire*
> *leave your trickery behind*
> *go insane*
> *go mad*
> *burn like a candle-moth*

The tangible and the intangible essence of
"Fire" is touched by Rumi far beyond what his
holy books and holy men have touched, or even
allowed to be touched.

> *my soul is a kiln*
> *happy with fire*
> *it suffices for a kiln*
> *to be the house of fire*

> *if you're in doubt*
> *of my flame*
> *touch your face*
> *with my face*
> *for a moment*

* Hundreds of books and papers have been written about Rumi's life and work. Recently, some of the best in English are: Annemarie Schimmel, *I Am Wind, You Are Fire: The Life and Work of Rumi* (Boston: Shambhala, 1992); also *The Triumphal Sun: A Study of the Works of Jalaloddin Rumi* (London:East-West publications, 1978); William C.Chittick, *The Sufi Path of Love: The Spiritual Teachings of Rumi* (Albany: SUNY Press, 1983); also *Rumi and the Mawlawiyya*, in S.H.Nasr (ed.), *Islamic Spirituality: Manifestation* (New York: Crossroad, 1991), pp.105-126.

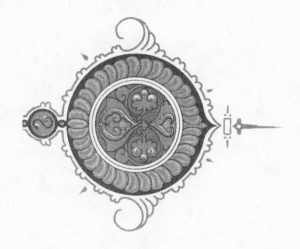

Rumi,

DREAMS OF RUMI

My grandmother, who could hardly read or write, yet knew by heart hundreds of Persian poems, including many of Rumi's love poems and short stories, inspired and instilled in me the celebration of life, love, and death in rhyme. And in adult life as an architect fired by a quest, spending twenty-five years in the deserts of Iran and California, I have come to know five personalities very closely: Earth, Water, Air, Fire, and Rumi. Rumi gave me the ultimate answer for my Archemy, architecture and alchemy, on earth, on the moon, Mars and beyond: Water is fire, earth is water, and there is a unity in all elements.

I have also discovered, dealing with these universal elements for my own earth-and-fire architecture, that Rumi, more than any other individual has dealt with fire and water, or earth and wind, and yet no one to my knowledge has looked at Rumi's life and works through these elements. I have been blessed by making my life's work following this narrow stream springing from the ocean that is Rumi.

In the last seven hundred years many millions have lit their candles from Rumi's fire and I feel I am one of them - awake or dreaming.

And thus the grace of his appearing in my dreams continued as my praying to know the secrets of his words continues for the last quarter of century.

Dancing the Flame

In this recurring dream I am walking on a sidewalk on the right hand of a street. The sidewalk is wide, asphalted, and has rows of shops along the way curving to the right. Several other people are also present at this time and walking independently. As I walk forward I hear a voice behind me calling me "Rumi, Rumi," but I don't turn back to look. I think "whoever it is calling must be exaggerating. I cannot be the Moulana Jalaloddin Rumi. He was an ultimate soul, a much greater person than I can ever be".

When I hear this voice I wake up. I remember that this is the same sidewalk which I dreamt I was walking on, several years ago when I saw Rumi and was blessed with an encounter and an intimate conversation. But what was different in that dream is that I was walking from east to west, and in this dream I am walking from west to east.*

Amidst many seemingly unrelated dreams in previous months and lately sobering thoughts that a new stage in life is beginning to surface, the following dream arrives:

In this dream I am in a room and I know that it is in the time of Jalaloddin Rumi. I don't see anything on the walls or in the surroundings to indicate the place or time, but I know it is in his time and place. On my right, Rumi, same height as I, is standing wearing a greyish robe. He has no turban on his head. It seems that I had just arrived, yet I had been there for a long time. I say hello to him but as I am greeting him I remember that maybe I am being too casual with him and that was not right; I should have been more respectful and observant of his greatness. For this reason after saying hello, when he extends his hand, from under his now-black robe, to shake my hand, I shake his hands with both my hands, in today's Persian tradition as a of sign of respect. I bow my head and stand in silence. At the same time I think I should have kissed his hand, but it is too late since after shaking his hand I had stepped back one step.

---

* see "Rumi, Fountain of Fire" Dreams by the author

Rumi,

Then I notice all of a sudden that there are several people in the room. On Rumi's right several men are standing, I know they are the respected companions of Rumi. Two or three men further on is a thin man who is wearing a light blue robe. Now everybody is sitting; Rumi is sitting and I am also sitting. Then I am hesitant for a moment if this man in the light blue robe is Rumi and the one that I shook hands with is Dr. N. (a highly respected Iranian, Islamic, and Rumi scholar living in the U.S. today). Anyhow, Rumi is there and the man in the light blue robe says that "with the 2 Rials (2 Pennies) that we have given to T. he can start a business for himself. Having said that both Rumis shake their head in agreement (T. was a previous student of mine in architecture, a native American young man from the Navajo Nation, that later became architect and we have kept our friendship. The rial is today's Iranian currency, a coin similar to a penny). Every one seems to agree that 2 Rials is sufficient money to start a business. They all laugh and a happy and friendly conversation begins amongst everybody in the room, and I wake up.

Another dream came several months later . It took place at the Cal-Earth Institute site in Mojave desert where our first Rumi Dome of Lights is constructed. This dream arrived the night before Dr. S. (a popular Persian poetry teacher and scholar) and his Rumi students, about thirty men and women, come up to the high desert to visit and have a Rumi poetry session in the Rumi Dome of Lights. They were coming for the first time and, except for one couple, I had not met any one of them before.

In this dream I see that all the visitors are wearing the same color uniform, navy blue trousers and light blue shirts. They are all young and have well shaped sportsman-like bodies, and in this scene they are standing in line and I am shaking hands with each one and greet them individually. When I reach the last one I see that his face is turned looking in the other direction. He is wearing no uniform, but instead he is very casually dressed. At this point I notice that I, too, am wearing a short trousers and sandals and compared to the others I am not as clean and appropriately dressed. Looking at the last man and seeing him smile I recognize that he is an old friend of mine, always with joyous loud laughter, whom I hadn't seen for many years. I gently touch his face with my hand, say hello, ask how he is, and we hug as good old friends. Suddenly I notice that he isn't my old friend as I thought but is Rumi himself. Then again, in moments the scene changes and I see myself as Rumi and my friend standing in front of me shaking hands with me and we both are laughing aloud. And I wake up.

The next day when the poetry teacher and his students arrive I tell them the dream, except for the last part which I feel shy to talk about. We have a happy and inspiring day with the home cooking they bring and the exchange of Rumi poems in the dome. On that day, just a little while before they arrive, a totally strange visitor travelling from Arizona to California arrived. He came to our site to ask if he could play his designed and carved African based musical instrument in the Rumi Dome of Lights. As he begins playing, the poetry group arrives and we all join in the dome and carry on the Rumi poetry session in the original Persian language. Everyone feels delighted listening to the guest's playing his instrument. Though he didn't know any Persian, to our bewilderment, all along he knew what we have been talking about and reciting. "I am only a lover of Rumi's mystic poetry and no more," he said.

The other dream relates to a long time before that and it came not to me but to my youngest sister, to whom I had always been very close.

This has happened before, whenever I have been crowded in life my dreams have gone to her. At the time of this dream I was designing, constructing, and teaching in the small semi-desert town of New Cuyyama, California. One of the projects was a thirty foot diameter Rumi Dome of Lights, which we were constructing out of un-fired clay brick; we later fired and ceramic glazed the structure entirely. The interior of the dome had graphics and calligraphy of some of Rumi's poems. The dome floor was covered with colorful Navajo sand-paintings to be fired and glazed along with the structure. The dome was destroyed before its second firing by one of the project's partners. Now on this large site there was a white spherical shape, and very tall water tank standing on a central column. My sister's dream of Rumi dealt with this tower. She wrote:

"I am in New Cuyyama and I see Rumi, very tall, standing behind the water tank and when he sees me approaching he bends down and gives me a thick book and says 'give this to Nader and tell him the poem he is looking for is in this book. There is a strand of hair marking the page. It may take a long time before you find that hair and that page, but you will eventually find it'. I only ask Rumi whether the strand of the hair is white or black. Rumi says that he (Nader) will know it himself. And I wake up.

Rumi's hair in my dream was white and his body was as tall as the water tank. It seemed that when he wanted to talk to me he would bring out his head at the top, bend down to talk to me, then would go and hide behind the water tank".

Many years later and I am still looking for that page marked with a strand of Rumi's hair.

In August of 2000 I went on a pilgrimage to Rumi's shrine to choose and translate the last few poems in the shrine and finish the translations of these Rubaiyat which I had started six years earlier. The collection was destined to end with the first poem I saw, a Rubaii, calligraphed and hung on the shrine's wall as I entered the blessed space:

> **come**
> whoever you are
> come
> come again
> even if you are godless
> and a worshipper of
> fire and idols
> come
> our home is the home of
> never losing hope
> come
> even if you break
> your repentance vows
> a hundred times
> come again
> come

Entering Rumi's shrine I had the manuscript as well as these dreams written down in Persian, including the one in my sister's own hand writing, with me. I was seeking Rumi's permission to end this little book and to share with others.

In this pilgrimage I was also searching to find traces of something more than a museum piece, that is alive and tangible from Rumi's time, even more permanent and untouched than the handful of holy earth of the shrine that I would be bringing back. I prayed for any gift that holds Rumi's energy, Rumi's soul, something I could touch and even photograph to bring back as a gift for my friends. As our all night bus ride was reaching the outskirts of the city of Konya, the sun, Rumi's sun, Shams, was rising: One dawn, a glorious dawn.

By the time we reached the shrine I had no doubt that this small book must begin with dawn: One dawn. And I shall only photograph the light, the sources of light, a gift right from Rumi's time. And no more.

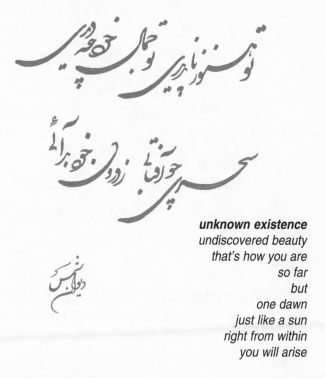

unknown existence
undiscovered beauty
that's how you are
so far
but
one dawn
just like a sun
right from within
you will arise

Rumi,

NOTE ON TRANSLATION

These non-literal translations of "Rubaiyat" quatrains and a few other lines from the book of the Diwan-i Shams-i Tabrizi are taken from the tenth Persian edition of Furuzanfar . The last lines are from Rumi's shrine, (though some don't agree with the original source).

The numbered poems correspond with Furuzanfar's numbered Rubaiyat in Persian and are listed in the index. As Rumi says, he had recited Rubaiyat amidst other love poems; here separating them from other forms of poems is merely respecting the Persian tradition of introducing poems in their indigenous casting forms, such as Ghazal, Rubaiyat, (quatrains) and others.

Like his original poems in Persian, I have tried to eliminate all punctuation marks. I would have eliminated my own name as a translator if it were possible at this juncture as Rumi never mentions his own real name in his entire book.

I have presented these poems* in series according to the date of their translation from 1994 to the year 2,000, as they came to me. Searching and choosing of these specific poems corresponds with the events of my life, and the dreams of the time. By writing down some of my Rumi related dreams I merely mean to report them rather than imply any interpretation. Many a time I have chosen a specific poem or a group of them (both in Rumi, Fountain of Fire and the present book) by looking for a specific letter, word, or meaning coming to me. Following that inspiration I then have gone to the index of the Persian origin (which is traditionally organized according to the last letter of the last word of the first line of the poem). To keep this mystic path open in the translated text, a dear friend suggested that the reader can also enter the poems in this manner:

Choose one letter of the alphabet or a word coming to your heart or mind, use that as the doorway to a poem, then refer to the index at the end of this book. Select one of the poems by its number and then read.

---

* A draft of this book was first presented as a commemorative pre-publication copy for the Rumi 2,000 Festival at California State University (UCSB), where Nader Khalili was the opening keynote speaker.

Rumi,

Index

Rumi,

Rubaiyat first line	Furuzanfar#	Poem#

I

i am happy	1115	78
i am happy with	1321	130
i am happy with a wine	1319	129
i am in love with love	1516	104
i am ready to bow	1338	138
i am so close to you	1121	18
i am the one with hunger	1350	146
i am the whole sea	1329	133
i asked a person	580	293
i asked my mentor	1680	112
i break all the rules	1347	264
i came to this world	31	35
i cannot be at peace	592	296
i can't choose anyone	1346	144
i can't get together	1494	102
i can't let you know	1141	29
i don't imagine	500	274
i don't really need wine	97	63
i have a tongue	403	207
i have become	1351	147
i have gone crazy	336	220
i haven't lost hope	1974	170
i imagine marching	44	59
i know of a path	185	7
i know the habits	1341	140
i only see myself	1110	12
i saw unhappiness	1909	180
i say to the night	197	246
i see healing	1131	73
i seek fire	1133	87
i seek my beloved	1154	74
i shall talk to you	222	8
i tell my heart	88	60
i thought if my lust	1295	259
i told you don't sit	1504	100

Rubaiyat first line	Furuzanfar#	Poem#
i took a journey	1854	90
i used to be wise and clever	1354	149
i was a pious preacher	1891	294
i was first seduced by love	14	33
i was in rage	1175	28
i went to the doctor	1479	83
i wish i knew	1752	19
i wish much grief	537	279
i wish you happiness	601	298
i wouldn't exchange	1334	135
if for the span of	1933	177
if i only knew	1925	179
if there is no fire	370	210
if you desire to see	1847	162
if you don't keep company	1674	108
if you fall behind	1977	171
if you gorge yourself	1929	175
if you reach for a star	1817	91
if you really knew	1715	199
if you see me getting old	1332	134
if you seek eternity	109	68
if you seek this world	1749	193
if you take this	572	290
if you want to be happy	1564	17
if you want to find yourself	62	47
if you won't fall in love	988	203
if you're a seeker	1502	98
if you're happy	1849	161
if you're hunted by God	1921	178
if you're with everyone	1793	190
i'll leap a hundred stages	754	119
i'm a speck of dust	71	51
i'm a spinner in dance	1349	145
i'm a stranger to be	238	9
i'm like someone who is	1355	150
i'm no more just a creature	1135	75

Rumi,

Dancing the Flame

Rubaiyat first line	Furuzanfar#	Poem#
M		
make sure you won't regret	*1802*	**188**
make your journeys	*355*	**214**
Mansour was the man	*72*	**52**
many are sad	*369*	**209**
my beautiful friend	*90*	**61**
my dear friend	*1739*	**195**
my dear heart hope	*1105*	**43**
my dear heart keep	*554*	**284**
my dear heart please	*1406*	**158**
my dear heart there is	*349*	**217**
my dear heart you can't	*553*	**283**
my dear heart you really	*1731*	**194**
my dear heart you'll	*524*	**275**
my essence is the essence	*9*	**2**
my God you are a trap	*1725*	**197**
my life was	*1975*	**93**
my sweetheart	*1109*	**10**
N		
never say	*729*	**72**
night again	*745*	**97**
no one exists in this world	*1503*	**99**
no way i'll let anyone	*1335*	**136**
now and then	*1325*	**128**
now that you've stolen	*531*	**277**
O		
o love	*558*	**286**
one day this blooming	*1759*	**192**
out of this world	*257*	**231**
out there you'll find	*1810*	**22**
P		
pain and pain and pain	*1482*	**84**

Rumi,

Rubaiyat first line	Furuzanfar#	Poem#

R

recite a poem	1557	256
remembrance of God	529	276
rise o day	556	285

S

searching for love	1301	258
seek only the knowledge	106	67
since God had written	43	44
since i have learned	1322	131
smile at every human	578	292
someone's hands	48	58
sweetheart i see myself	25	34

T

take me in my love	1408	25
that eternal candle	1490	101
the cry of the viol's music	1712	200
the day i distill to a sea	6	4
the day love	482	266
the day my soul	479	265
the days you seem to be	1661	79
the drum begs for	1360	153
the moon is rising	1357	152
the mystery hidden	347	218
the one who	490	271
the one who has	133	254
the one you know me	216	238
the other day	1880	183
the pal within you	218	237
the sweetheart	3	3
the sweetheart in my dream	1964	14
the world is luscious green	1903	182
there are two attitudes	1305	261
there is a passage	337	216
there is a soul	45	45

Rumi,

Rubaiyat first line	Furuzanfar#	Poem#
you wrote a message	*1561*	**16**
you'll arrive to	*1666*	**110**
you'll be smart and alert	*1679*	**201**
your home is	*1771*	**191**
your imagination my friend	*1721*	**198**
your love is	*1344*	**143**
your lover may seem timid	*760*	**122**
your soul and mine	*1566*	**23**
you're committing	*1798*	**186**
you're crawling in a corner	*1409*	**159**
you're fulfilled	*273*	**228**
you're in my eyes otherwise	*1857*	**165**
you're like a flower	*1950*	**173**
you're not earth	*1821*	**184**
you're so stuck	*223*	**236**
you're super perfection	*1343*	**142**
you've finally filled the	*1675*	**76**

Dancing the Flame